YORUBA LEGENDS

BY
M. I. OGUMEFU

Contents

Preface

1. The Kingdom Of The Yorubas
2. How Tribal Marks Came To Be Used
3. Akiti The Hunter
4. Sons Of Sticks
5. Why Women Have Long Hair
6. Why People Cry "Long Live The King!" When Thunder Follows Lightning
7. The Olofin And The Mice
8. The Iroko Tree
9. Orisa Oko
10. Moremi
11. The Bat
12. The Leopard-Man
13. The Water-Bird
14. The Ants And The Treasure
15. The Voices Of Birds
16. The Three Magicians
17. Isokun And The Baby
18. The Twin Brothers
19. How Leopard Got His Spots
20. Another Story Of Leopard's Spots
21. The Head
22. Ole And The Ants
23. The Boa-Constrictor
24. Oluronbi
25. The Staff Of Oranyan
26. The Elephant's Trunk

27. The Secret Of The Fishing-Baskets
28. The Ten Goldsmiths
29. The Cooking-Pot
30. The Parrot
31. The Ghost-Catcher
32. Tortoise And The King
33. Tortoise And Mr. Fly
34. Erin And Erinomi (The Land And Water Elephants)
35. The Three Deaths Of Tortoise
36. Tortoise And The Cock
37. Tortoise And Crab
38. Tortoise And Pigeon
39. Tortoise And The Whip-Tree
40. Tortoise And The Rain

Preface

IN modern times we have begun paying close attention to folklore—old tales, not invented by one man, but belonging to the whole people; not written down, but told by parents to their children, and so handed on for hundreds of years.

The legends and fairy stories in this book belong to the Yoruba country of Southern Nigeria. They relate the adventures of men and animals, and try to explain the mysteries of Nature—Why Women have Long Hair, How the Leopard got his Spots, and so forth. Most of them include very old songs, but these cannot here be given in full.

We must not think that the stories are scientifically true; they grew out of the imagination of the people, and for actual, proven facts we must look in our text-books. We read these folk-tales for their quaintness and humour, for their sympathy with Nature, and because we find in them the ideas and ideals, not just of one man, but of the race.

The legends express primitive notions of right and wrong, and in this they fall below the new standard which Christianity has set for our actions. As a rule, however, the wicked are punished and the good rewarded; and that, we feel, is as it should be. We may weep at the death of rascally Tortoise, but we feel that he deserves his fate!

1. THE KINGDOM OF THE YORUBAS

THE ancient King Oduduwa had a great many grandchildren, and on his death he divided among them all his possessions. But his youngest grandson, Oranyan, was at that time away hunting, and when he returned home he learnt that his brothers and cousins had inherited the old King's money, cattle, beads, native cloths, and crowns, but that to himself nothing was left but twenty-one pieces of iron, a cock, and some soil tied up in a rag.

At that time the whole earth was covered with water, on the surface of which the people lived.

The resourceful Oranyan spread upon the water his pieces of iron, and upon the iron he placed the scrap of cloth, and upon the cloth the soil, and on the soil the cock.

The cock scratched with his feet and scattered the soil far and wide, so that the ocean was partly filled up and islands appeared everywhere. The pieces of iron became the mineral wealth hidden under the ground.

Now Oranyan's brothers and cousins all desired to live on the land, and Oranyan allowed them to do so on payment of tribute. He thus became King of all the Yorubas, and was rich and prosperous through his grandfather's inheritance.

2. How Tribal Marks Came To Be Used

A CERTAIN King named Sango sent two slaves to a distant country on an important mission.

In due course they returned, and he found that one slave had achieved successfully what he had been sent to do, while the other had accomplished nothing.

The King therefore rewarded the first with high honours, and commanded the second to receive a hundred and twenty-two razor cuts all over his body.

This was a severe punishment, but when the scars healed, they gave to the slave a very remarkable appearance, which greatly took the fancy of the King's wives.

Sango therefore decided that cuts should in future be given, not as punishment, but as a sign of royalty, and he placed himself at once in the hands of the markers. However, he could only bear two cuts, and so from that day two cuts on the arm have been the sign of royalty, and various other cuts came to be the marks of different tribes.

3. Akiti The Hunter

A FAMOUS hunter and wrestler named Akiti boasted that he was stronger than any other man or animal. He had easily overcome a giant, a leopard, a lion, a wolf, and a boa-constrictor, and as nobody else opposed his claim, he called himself "the King of the forest."

Wherever he went, he sang his triumphant wrestling-song, and everyone feared and respected him. But he had forgotten the Elephant, who is a very wise animal and knows many charms. One day the Elephant challenged him and declared that he had no right to call himself "King," as the Elephant himself was the monarch of the forest and could not be defeated.

Akiti thereupon flung his spear at his enemy, but because of the Elephant's charm, the weapon glanced off his hide and did him no harm. Akiti next tried his bow and poisoned arrows, and his hunting-knife, but still without effect.

However, the hunter also possessed a charm, and by using it, he changed himself into a lion and flew at the Elephant, but the Elephant flung him off. Next he became a serpent, but he could not succeed in crushing the Elephant to death.

At last he changed himself into a fly, and flew into the Elephant's large flapping ear. He went right down inside until he came to the heart, and then he changed himself into a man again and cut up the heart with his hunting-knife. At last the Elephant fell dead, and Akiti stepped out of his body in triumph, for he was now without question "the King of the forest."

4. Sons Of Sticks

A GREAT King sent his various sons to rule over different parts of his kingdom, and all were satisfied but one, the youngest and most ambitious, who returned to his father after some time with the complaint that his territory was much too small and his subjects too few.

The King was displeased with his son, and sent for a large bundle of sticks, which he converted into human beings.

"Here are some more subjects for you!" he said to the astonished Prince.

From that time the tribe was famous for its strength and stupidity, and went by the nickname of "Sons of Sticks," or "Ọmọ igi"!

5. WHY WOMEN HAVE LONG HAIR

TWO women quarrelled, and one of them went out secretly at night and dug a deep pit in the middle of the path leading from her enemy's house to the village well.

Early next morning, when all were going to the well for water with jars balanced on their heads, this woman fell into the pit and cried loudly for help.

Her friends ran to her and, seizing her by the hair, began to pull her out of the pit. To their surprise, her hair stretched as they pulled, and by the time she was safely on the path, her hair was as long as a man's arm.

This made her very much ashamed, and she ran away and hid herself.

But after a while she realized that her long hair was beautiful, and then she felt very proud and scorned all the short-haired women, jeering at them. When they saw this, they were consumed with jealousy, and began to be ashamed of their short hair. "We have men's hair," they said to one another. "How beautiful it would be to have long hair!"

So one by one they jumped into the pit, and their friends pulled them out by the hair.

And in this way they, and all women after them, had long hair.

6. Why People Cry "Long Live The King!" When Thunder Follows Lightning

KING SANGO was acquainted with many deadly charms, and he once happened to discover a preparation by which he could attract lightning.

He foolishly decided to try the effect of the charm first of all on his own palace, which was at the foot of a hill.

Ascending the hill with his courtiers, the King employed the charm: a storm suddenly arose, the palace was struck by lightning and burnt to the ground, together with Sango's whole family.

Overcome with grief at having lost his possessions, and above all his sons, the impetuous King resolved to retire to a corner of his kingdom and to rule no more. Some of his courtiers agreed with him, and others tried to dissuade him from the plan; but Sango in his rage executed a hundred and sixty of them—eighty who had disagreed with him, and eighty who had agreed too eagerly!

Then, accompanied by a few friends, he left the place and started on his long journey. One by one his friends deserted him on the way, until he was left alone, and in despair he decided to put an end to his life, which he rashly did.

When they heard of the deed, his people came to the spot and gave him an honourable funeral, and he was ever afterwards worshipped as the god of thunder and lightning. So, among all the Yorubas, when people see the flash of lightning followed by the sullen roar of thunder, they remember Sango's rage after the destruction of his palace, and exclaim: "Long live the King!"

7. The Olofin And The Mice

A FAMOUS Olofin, or Yoruba King, was once imprisoned by his enemies in a hut without any door or roof-opening, and left to die of starvation.

As he sat gloomily on the ground, the Olofin saw a little mouse running across the hut. He seized his knife, exclaiming: "Rather than die of hunger, I will eat this mouse!"

But on second thoughts he put away his knife, saying: "Why should I kill the mouse? I shall starve later on, just the same."

To his surprise the mouse addressed him in the following words:

"Noble King! Greetings to you on your generosity! You have spared my life, and in return I will spare yours."

The mouse then disappeared into a hole in the ground, and returned some time afterwards followed by twenty or thirty other mice, all bearing grains of corn, gari, and small fruits.

For five days they fed him in this manner, and on the sixth day the hut was opened by the Olofin's captors, who were astonished to find him still alive and in good health.

"This Olofin must have a powerful charm!" they declared. "It appears that he can live without eating or drinking!"

Thereupon they released him, gave him a war-canoe, and let him return in freedom to his own country.

---

8. The Iroko Tree

IN the forest there is a giant tree called by the Yorubas the "Iroko," which is shunned by all people, for in it lives the spirit of an old man who prowls about at night with a little torch and frightens travellers.

Anyone who sees the Iroko-man face to face goes mad and speedily dies.

Seeing the thick branches and mighty trunk of the Iroko, woodcutters are often tempted to cut the tree down and make use of the wood, but this is very unlucky, as it rouses the displeasure of the Iroko-man and brings misfortune on the woodcutter and all his family.

In any house which contains furniture made of Iroko-wood, there can be heard at night strange groaning and creaking noises; it is the spirit of the Iroko, imprisoned in the wood, who longs to wander about again through the forest with his little torch.

9. Orisa Oko

ORISA OKO was a poor hunter, solitary save for his fife and his dog. If ever he lost his way out in the fields or the forest, he would begin to play some plaintive melody on his fife, and the sounds would lead the faithful dog to his side to guide him home.

He earned a meagre living by trapping in his nets guinea-fowls on the land of rich farmers, but because of his solitary life and his habit of silence, he was respected as a man possessed of secret knowledge which he did not care to divulge.

As years went by, he grew too old for hunting, and took up his residence in a cave. People now thought him more mysterious than ever, and came to him for advice about the future, so that in a short time he won great renown as a soothsayer. From far and near people came to consult him, and in this way he managed to live very comfortably.

In those days witchcraft was punished by death, and it became the custom in the country that anyone suspected of the evil art should be dragged to Orisa Oko's cave. If the soothsayer found him innocent, he led him forth by the hand, but if he were judged guilty, his head was cut off and thrown to the waiting crowd by the demon Polo, which Orisa Oko kept in the cave.

This went on until the old hunter's death. His followers now wished to continue the practice, and so they hid in the cave a very strong man to act as the demon Polo. When anyone accused of witchcraft was brought to the cave, his head was usually cut off and thrown out as before.

However, it once happened that a very tall and muscular man was suspected of magic arts, and his accusers succeeded in dragging him to the cave.

A large crowd waited with eagerness to learn the result. What was their dismay to see the head of the supposed "demon" come rolling out of the cave, for the strong man had proved too much for him, and soon reappeared unharmed and triumphant.

The people were indignant to learn how they had been deceived, and from that day the cave of Orisa Oko was deserted.

10. MOREMI

A NOBLEMAN of Ile-Ife had a beautiful and virtuous wife named Moremi, and a handsome young son, Ela.

The country of the Ifes was at that time subject to fierce raids by a tribe called the Igbos, who were of such an uncanny appearance in battle that the Ifes thought them not human, but a visitation sent by the gods in punishment for some evil. In vain did they offer sacrifices to the gods; the raids of these strange beings continued, and the land was thrown into a state of pamc.

Now the heroic Moremi, desiring to bring an end to this condition of affairs, resolved to let herself be captured during one of the raids, so that she might be carried as a prisoner to the land of the Igbos and learn all their secrets.

Bidding farewell to her husband and her little son, she went to a certain stream and promised the god of the stream that, if her attempt was successful, she would offer to him the richest sacrifice she could afford.

As she had planned, she was captured by the Igbos and carried away to their capital as a prisoner. On account of her beauty she was given to the King of the Igbos as a slave; and on account of her intelligence and noble heart she soon gained the respect of all and rose to a position of importance.

Before she had been in the country very long, she had learnt all the secrets of her enemies. She found that they were not gods but ordinary men. On going into battle they wore strange mantles of grass and bamboo fibre, and this accounted for their unnatural appearance. She also learned that because of these mantles of dry grass, they were much afraid of fire, and that if the Ifes were to rush among them with lighted torches, they would quickly be defeated. As soon as it was possible, she escaped from the palace and from the territory of the Igbos and returned to her own people. Her tidings were joyfully received at Ile-Ife, and shortly afterwards the Igbos were utterly defeated by the trick Moremi had suggested.

Moremi now went to the stream and made a great sacrifice of sheep, fowls, and bullocks; but the god of the stream was not satisfied and demanded the life of her son.

Sorrowing, Moremi was forced to consent, and sacrificed the handsome boy Ela. The Ifes wept to see this sad spectacle, and they promised to be her sons and daughters for ever, to make up for her loss.

But lo! Ela as he lay upon the ground was only half dead, and when the people had departed, he recovered consciousness and sprang up. Making a rope of grass, he climbed up to heaven, and it is certain that he will some day return to reap the benefits of his mother's noble sacrifice.

11. The Bat

THE Bat is half a bird and half a rodent, and lives partly on the earth and partly in the air, but both rats and birds shun him, and this is why:

The rats, his cousins, were once fighting a great battle with the birds, and Bat fought in their midst.

But when he saw that the birds were likely to be victorious, he left the rats and flew up into the air to fight on the side of the birds.

Both the rats and the birds were disgusted at this cowardly action, so they ceased from fighting one another and all combined to attack the Bat.

Since that day he has been forced to hide in dark places all day, and only comes out in the evening when his enemies cannot see him.

12. The Leopard-Man

A HANDSOME stranger once came into a certain village and strolled about among the people in mysterious silence. All the maidens admired him and wished that he would choose one of them for his bride. But he said nothing, and at last walked away into the forest and disappeared from sight.

A month later the stranger came again, and this time one of the maidens fell so much in love with him that she resolved to follow him into the forest, as she could not bear to be separated from him.

When the stranger looked back and saw her coming behind him, he stopped, and begged her to return home; but she would not, and exclaimed: "I will never leave you, and wherever you go, I will follow."

"Beautiful maiden, you will regret it," replied the stranger sadly, as he hurried on.

After a while he stopped again, and once more begged her to retrace her steps; but she made the same reply, and again the handsome stranger said in sorrowful tones: "You will regret it, beautiful maiden!"

They went far into the depths of the forest, and at length reached a tree at the foot of which there lay a leopard-skin. Standing under the tree, the stranger began to sing a melancholy song, in which he told her that though he was allowed once a month to wander about in villages and towns like a man, he was in reality a savage leopard and would rend her in pieces as soon as he regained his natural form.

With these words he flung himself upon the ground, and immediately became a snarling leopard and began to pursue the terrified girl.

But fear gave such speed to her feet that he could not overtake her. As he pursued her he sang that he would tear her in small pieces, and she in another song replied that he would never overtake her.

For a great distance they ran, and then the maiden suddenly came to a deep but narrow river, which she could not cross. It seemed as if the leopard would catch her after all. But a tree, which stood on the river-bank, took pity on her and fell across the river, so that she was able to cross.

At last, nearly exhausted, she came to the edge of the forest and reached the village in safety. The leopard, disappointed of its prey, slunk back into the forest, and the handsome stranger was never seen again.

---

13. THE WATER-BIRD

THE water-bird always stands on one leg, and this is why:

A water-bird once, in search of food, swallowed the King of the crabs, and the whole tribe of crabs were so enraged that they swore they would have their revenge.

"We will find this horrible bird," they declared, "and nip off its legs. We shall not fail to find it, for its legs are bright pink in colour and its feathers are pink and white."

But the water-rat overheard the crabs plotting, and hastened to tell the water-bird.

"Oh! Oh!" cried the water-bird. "They will nip off my beautiful pink legs, and then what will become of me? Whatever can I do?"

"It is very simple," replied the water-rat. "If you stand on one leg, they will think you are some other creature."

The bird thanked him and tucked up one leg. When the crabs came, they saw, as they thought, a very tall pink bird with one leg and a large beak.

"Our enemy has two legs," they said. "This cannot be he." And they passed by.

14. The Ants And The Treasure

THERE once was a poor man who was very kind to animals and birds. However little he had, he always spared a few grains of corn, or a few beans, for his parrot, and he was in the habit of spreading on the ground every morning some titbits for the industrious ants, hoping that they would be satisfied with the corn and leave his few possessions untouched.

And for this the ants were grateful.

In the same village there lived a miser who had by crafty and dishonest means collected a large store of gold, which he kept securely tied up in the corner of a small hut. He sat outside this hut all day and all night, so that nobody could steal his treasure.

When he saw any bird, he threw a stone at it, and he crushed any ant which he found walking on the ground, for he detested every living creature and loved nothing but his gold.

As might be expected, the ants had no love for this miser, and when he had killed a great many of their number, they began to think how they might punish him for his cruelty.

"What a pity it is," said the King of the ants, "that our friend is a poor man, while our enemy is so rich!"

This gave the ants an idea. They decided to transfer the miser's treasure to the poor man's house. To do this they dug a great tunnel under the ground. One end of the tunnel was in the poor man's house, and the other end was in the hut of the miser.

On the night that the tunnel was completed, a great swarm of ants began carrying the miser's treasure into the poor man's house, and when morning came and the poor man saw the gold lying in heaps on the floor, he was overjoyed, thinking that the gods had sent him a reward for his years of humble toil.

He put all the gold in a corner of his hut and covered it up with native cloths.

Meanwhile the miser had discovered that his treasure was greatly decreased. He was alarmed and could not think how the gold could have disappeared, for he had kept watch all the time outside the hut.

The next night the ants again carried a great portion of the miser's gold down the tunnel, and again the poor man rejoiced and the miser was furious to discover his loss.

On the third night the ants laboured long and succeeded in removing all the rest of the treasure.

"The gods have indeed sent me much gold!" cried the poor man, as he put away his treasure.

But the miser called together his neighbours and related that in three consecutive nights his hard-won treasure had vanished away. He declared that nobody had entered the hut but himself, and therefore the gold must have been removed by witchcraft.

However, when the hut was searched, a hole was found in the ground, and they saw that this hole was the opening of a tunnel. It seemed clear that the treasure had been carried down the tunnel, and everyone began hunting for the other end of the tunnel. At last it was discovered in the poor man's hut! Under the native cloths in the corner they found the missing treasure.

The poor man protested in vain that he could not possibly have crept down such a small tunnel, and he declared that he had no notion how the gold had got into his but. But the rest said that be must have some charm by which he made himself very small and crept down the tunnel at night into the miser's hut.

For this offence they shut him up in a hut and tightly closed the entrance. On the next day he was to be burnt alive.

When the ants saw what had come of their plan to help him, they were sorely perplexed and wondered how they could save their poor friend from such a painful death

There seemed nothing for them to do but to eat up the whole of the hut where the prisoner was confined. This they accomplished after some hours, and the poor man was astonished to find himself standing in an open space. He ran away into the forest and never came back.

In the morning the people saw that the ants had been at work, for a few stumps of the hut remained. They said: "The gods have taken the punishment out of our hands! The ants have devoured both the hut and the prisoner!"

And only the ants knew that this was not true.

---

15. The Voices Of Birds

A MAGICIAN once passed through a grove in the forest where a great many brown birds fluttered from tree to tree and filled the air with songs. For a long time he sat and listened, enraptured by their beautiful melodies, but in the end he became very jealous, for he himself could not sing.

At last he felt that he must by some means or other possess the voices of these singing birds, so he called them all together and said:

"It grieves me that the gods have given you all such poor, ugly brown feathers. How happy you would be if you were brilliantly coloured with red, blue, orange, and green!"

And the birds agreed that it was a great pity to be so ugly.

The magician then suggested that by means of his charms he could give them all beautiful feathers in exchange for their voices—which were, after all, of very little use to them, since nobody came into the grove to hear them.

The birds thought over his words, and desired very much the beauty he promised them. So they foolishly agreed to give him their voices, which the magician placed all together in a large calabash. He then used his charms to turn the dull brown feathers of the birds into orange and green and red, and they were very pleased.

The magician hurried away, and as soon as he came to a deserted place he opened the calabash and swallowed its contents. From that day he had an exceedingly sweet voice, and people came from far and near to listen to his songs.

But the birds were satisfied with their bright feathers. And this is why the most beautiful birds are quite unable to sing.

16. The Three Magicians

A CERTAIN King had engaged in a series of wars, during which he employed three magicians or medicine-men to make charms for him, so that he might destroy his enemies.

At the end of the war these three magicians came to the King and humbly asked to be allowed to return home. The King foolishly refused, and at this the magicians said:

"We asked your permission out of courtesy, O King, but we can very easily depart without it."

Thereupon the first magician fell down on the ground and disappeared. The second threw a ball of twine into the air, climbed up the thread and disappeared likewise. The third magician, Elenre, remained standing.

"It is your turn to disappear," said the King, trembling with anger, "or I will slay you."

"You cannot harm me," replied the magician.

At this the King ordered him to be beheaded, but the sword broke in two, and the executioner's arm withered away. The King then ordered him to be speared, but the spear crumpled up and was useless. An attempt was made to crush the magician with a rock, but it rolled over his body as lightly as a child's ball.

The King then sent for the magician's wife and asked her to reveal his secret charm. At last the woman confessed that if they took one blade of grass from the thatched roof of a house, they could easily cut off his head with it.

This was done, and the magician's head rolled off and stuck to the King's hand. It could not by any means be removed. When food and drink was brought to the King, the head consumed it all, so that the King seemed likely to die.

Magicians were hastily summoned from all over the kingdom, but the head laughed at all their charms and remained fast.

Finally came one who prostrated himself before the head and cried out:

"Who am I to oppose you, great Elenre? I come only because the King commands me."

To this Elenre replied:

"You are wiser than all the rest!" and the head fell at once to the ground, where it became a flowing river, which to this day is called Odo Elenre, or Elenre's river.

The magician's wife was likewise changed into a river, but because she had betrayed him, Elenre commanded the river not to flow, and it became instead a stagnant pool.

---

17. Isokun And The Baby

A CERTAIN King Dekun had a wife named Isokun who bore him no children, on which account there was great unhappiness in the palace.

One day Isokun disappeared and was absent for many weeks, and though search was made, no trace of her could be found. The truth was that Isokun had set out to visit the shrines of all the gods, in the hope that one of them would promise her a child. But though she travelled far and wide, the gods of all the trees and streams and rocks refused her prayer.

When she was at last nearing home again, she came upon a poor woman asleep by the wayside with her baby two days old.

Isokun stole the baby and hastened to the palace, where she informed the King that she had disappeared in order to give him the joyous surprise of his little son.

There were great rejoicings in the palace, sacrifices were made, and the drums beat loudly.

Meanwhile the real mother awoke and discovered that her baby had been stolen.

She ran into the town distracted, and insisted on searching in every house, but without success.

At last she came to the palace and insisted on entering there also, which was possible at that moment because all were celebrating the arrival of the King's heir.

All this time the baby cried with hunger, and as Isokun could not feed him, she invented other reasons for the crying and sought in vain to pacify him without arousmg suspicion.

Drawn by the cries, the mother entered and snatched the baby to her breast, where it was at once contented.

In a few moments the deception was made clear, the mother departed with her child, and Isokun, ashamed and fearing the anger of the King, fled from the palace and never returned.

---

18. The Twin Brothers

A CERTAIN Yoruba King, Ajaka, had a favourite wife of whom he was very fond; but, alas for his hopes! she gave birth to twins.

At that time it was the universal custom to destroy twins immediately at birth, and the mother with them. But the King had not the heart to put this cruel law into execution, and he secretly charged one of his nobles to conduct the royal mother and her babes to a remote place where they might live in safety.

Here the twin brothers grew to manhood, and loved one another greatly. They were inseparable, and neither of them had any pleasure except in the company of the other. When one brother began to speak, the other completed his phrase, so harmonious were their thoughts and inclinations.

Their mother, before she died, informed them of their royal birth, and from this moment they spent the time vainly regretting their exile, and wishing that the law of the country had made it possible for them to reign.

At last they received the news that the King their father was dead, leaving no heir, and it seemed to the brothers that one of them ought to go to the capital and claim the throne. But which?

To settle this point they decided to cast stones, and the one who made the longer throw should claim the throne, and afterwards send for his brother to share in his splendour.

The lot fell on the younger of the twins, and he set off to the capital, announced himself as the Olọfin's son, and soon became King with the consent of all the people. As soon as possible he sent for his brother, who henceforth lived with him in the palace and was treated with honour and distinction.

But alas! jealousy began to overcome his brotherly affection, and one day as he walked with the King by the side of the river, he pushed his brother suddenly into the water, where he was drowned.

He then gave out in the palace that his brother was weary of kingship, and had left the country, desiring him to reign in his stead.

The King had certainly disappeared, and as no suspicion fell on the twin brother, he was made King and so realized his secret ambition.

Some time later, happening to pass by the very spot where his brother had been drowned, he saw a fish rise to the surface of the water and begin to sing:

> "Your brother lies here,
> Your brother lies here."

The King was very much afraid. He took up a sharp stone and killed the fish.

But another day when he passed the spot, attended by his nobles and shielded by the royal umbrella made of the skins of rare animals, the river itself rose into waves and sang:

> "Your brother lies here,
> Your brother lies here."

In astonishment the courtiers stopped to listen. Their suspicions were aroused, and when they looked into the water they found the body of the King.

Thus the secret of his disappearance was disclosed, and the wicked brother was rejected in horror by his people. At this disgrace he took poison and so died.

---

19. How Leopard Got His Spots

AT one time the Leopard was coloured like a lion, and he had no dark markings; but he was pursued by Akiti, the renowned hunter, and feared that he might be slain.

To avoid this he ate the roots of a certain magic plant, which had the effect of making him invulnerable to any of the hunter's weapons.

Soon afterwards Akiti saw him as he slipped through the dense undergrowth of the forest, but though he shot his poisoned arrows, Leopard escaped.

But where each arrow struck him, there appeared a dark mark, and now, though hunters still pursue him, he is rarely caught, but his body is covered with the marks of the arrows, so that as he goes among the trees he looks exactly like the mingling of the sun and shadow.

20. Another Story Of Leopard's Spots

ACCORDING to another story, Leopard once had a very dark skin. He was prowling one day in a beautiful compound, when he noticed a little hut in which a lady was taking her bath.

Round and round the hut Leopard walked, waiting for an opportunity to spring into the hut and seize his victim, for he was hungry.

But as he passed the opening of the hut, the lady saw him, and, uttering a scream of terror, she threw at him her loofah, which was full of soap.

> "She flung it at him and he fled,
> But to this day the Leopard still
> Is flecked with soap from foot to head!"

21. The Head

THERE is a certain country where the inhabitants have heads but no bodies. The Heads move about by jumping along the ground, but they never go very far.

One of the Heads desired to see the world, so he set out one morning secretly. When he had gone some distance, he saw an old woman looking out of the door of a hut, and he asked her if she would kindly lend him a body.

The old woman willingly lent him the body of her slave, and the Head thanked her and went on his way.

Later he came upon a young man sleeping under a tree, and asked him if he would kindly lend him a pair of arms, as he did not appear to be using them. The young man agreed, and the Head thanked him and went on his way.

Later still he reached a river-bank where fishermen sat singing and mending their cone-shaped net. The Head asked if any one of them would lend him a pair of legs, as they were all sitting and not walking. One of the fishermen agreed, and the Head thanked him and went on his way.

But now he had legs, arms, and a body, and so appeared like any other man.

In the evening he reached a town and saw maidens dancing while the onlookers threw coins to those they favoured. The Head threw all his coins to one of the dancers, and she so much admired his handsome form that she consented to marry him and go to live with him in his own country.

Next day they set out, but when they came to the river-bank, the stranger took off his legs and gave them back to the fisherman. Later they reached the young man, who still lay sleeping under the tree, and to him the Head gave back his arms. Finally they came to the cottage, where the old woman stood watching, and here the stranger gave up his body.

When the bride saw that her husband was merely a Head, she was filled with horror, and ran away as fast as she could go.

Now that the Head had neither body, arms, nor legs, he could not overtake her, and so lost her for ever.

22. Ole And The Ants

THERE was a certain lazy and disagreeable man whom everyone called "Ole," or "Lazy one." He liked to profit by the work of others, and was also very inquisitive about other people's affairs.

Once he saw that the ants had begun building a pillar in the compound of his house. But though the ants destroyed all the plants in the compound, and stripped all the trees, Ole would not trouble to kill them, or to break down their pillar.

Instead, he thought to himself: "When the ants have made this pillar very high, I will sit on the top of it, and then I shall be able to see all that my neighbours are doing without leaving my compound."

This thought pleased him, and he was glad that the ants swarmed in his compound. Each day the pillar grew higher, and at last the ants ceased their building and began again elsewhere. Ole then climbed up on to the pillar and spent the whole day observing the doings of his neighbours, and laughing at their activity.

> "Here sit I like a great Chief,
> And I see all things!"

sang Ole.

But while he sat on the pillar, the ants began to demolish his house and all that it contained, and in a short time there was nothing left of all his food and possessions.

Ole thus became the laughing-stock of the village, and everyone who saw him cried: "Ku ijoko!" or "Greetings to you on your sitting!"

Soon afterwards he died, and it is not known to this day whether he died of shame or of laziness.

23. The Boa-Constrictor

OGUNFUNMINIRE, the famous hunter, lived to such a great age that he was no longer able to go into the forest and chase the deer and the leopard.

Life had no other pleasure for him than hunting, so he went to a magician and asked for some charm which would enable him to continue his occupation.

The magician gave him two pots, each containing a charm. Every day Ogunfunminire dipped his head into the first pot and was at once transformed into a boa-constrictor, in which form he glided into the forest and hunted to his heart's content. At night he returned and dipped his head into the second pot, and so became a man again.

This went on for a long time without the knowledge of the old hunter's family, but when at last they chanced to discover the secret, they were filled with horror, and his son in a rage kicked at the pots and overturned them both.

Ogunfunminire was at that moment hunting in the forest, and when he returned to his house and found the magic pots overturned and empty, he was filled with dismay, for he had no means of regaining his human form. For some days the boa-constrictor glided about near the house, seeking for a few drops of the charm, but in vain, and at last he disappeared into the forest and was never seen by his family again.

24. Oluronbi

IN a certain village no children had been born for many years, and the people were greatly distressed.

At last all the women of the village went together into the forest, to the magic tree, the Iroko, and implored the spirit of the tree to help them.

The Iroko-man asked what gifts they would bring if he consented to help them, and the women eagerly promised him corn, yams, fruit, goats, and sheep; but Oluronbi, the young wife of a wood-carver, promised to bring her first child.

In due course children came to the village, and the most beautiful of all the children was the one born to Oluronbi. She and her husband so greatly loved their child that they could not consent to give it up to the Iroko-man.

The other women took their promised gifts of corn, yams, fruit, goats, and sheep; but Oluronbi took nothing to propitiate. the tree.

Alas! one day as Oluronbi passed through the forest, the Iroko-man seized her and changed her into a small brown bird, which sat on the branches of the tree and plaintively sang:

> "One promised a sheep,
> One promised a goat,
> One promised fruit,
> But Oluronbi promised her child."

When the wood-carver heard the bird's song, he realized what had happened, and tried to find some means of regaining his wife.

After thinking for many days, he began to carve a large wooden doll, like a real child in size and appearance, and with a small gold chain round its neck. Covering it with a beautiful native cloth, he laid it at the foot of the tree. The Iroko-man thought that this was Oluronbi's child, so he transformed the little bird once more into a woman and snatched up the child into the branches.

Oluronbi joyfully returned home, and was careful never to stray into the forest again.

---

25. The Staff Of Oranyan

ORANYAN, a brave and warlike King, founded the city of Oyo. As it was necessary for him to lead an expedition to a distant part of his kingdom, he left his son in charge of the capital during his absence.

But the King was away for such a long period that it was thought he and his soldiers must have perished, and at last the people made his son King, and for some time he ruled them wisely and happily.

However, Oranyan was not dead, and after many delays and hardships he again drew near to Oyo with his few surviving followers.

As he approached the city he was startled to hear the notes of the Kakaki trumpet, which is sounded for the King alone.

Feeling sure that nobody could be aware of his return, he asked a man working in the fields for whom the trumpet was being sounded.

"For the King," replied the man.

"Yes, but which King?" asked the travel-worn stranger.

"Do you not know that the son of Oranyan is King, and rules over us wisely and well? His father was killed in battle many months ago."

Desiring his son's happiness more than his own, the old King retraced his steps, and settled down with his few friends in humble retirement in a remote part of the country. Only at Oranyan's death was his presence made known to his son.

The young Prince, now King, grieving at his noble father's sacrifice, erected an obelisk over the spot where he died, and the monument, which is known as the Staff of Oranyan, is still to be seen.

26. The Elephant's Trunk

NOW it is a matter of common knowledge that Elephant has a long trunk, which he uses both as a nose and as a sort of hand—a very useful trunk indeed. But he was once without it, and had a very ordinary short snout like other animals.

Elephant was always inquisitive and went sniffing about the forest, prying into the secrets of the other animals. One day he came across a dark hole in the ground, and into this hole he poked his nose, to see what was there.

He at once regretted his curiosity, for a large snake, who lived in the hole, seized him by the nose and tried to swallow him. At this, Elephant made a great uproar, and his wife came rushing to his assistance. She seized his tail and pulled and pulled, and Elephant himself also pulled and pulled, but the snake would not leave go.

And as a result, Elephant's nose was drawn out into the long trunk which he still has.

At first he was ashamed to appear in the forest, on account of his trunk, but now the other animals envy him.

One day the monkey, which imitates everybody, looked down the same hole, thinking it would be good to have a long trunk so as to be able to swing from the trees by his nose. But the big snake who lived in the hole swallowed him, and since then nobody else has tried to imitate Elephant.

27. The Secret Of The Fishing-Baskets

ACROSS a certain river a poor fisherman set a row of stakes, and on each stake was fastened a basket in which he hoped to trap the fishes as they swam down the river.

But his luck was very bad, and every evening, as he went from basket to basket in his canoe, he was disappointed to find that no fishes, or only a few very small ones, had been caught.

This made him very sad, and he was forced to live frugally.

One day he found a stranger lying asleep on the river-bank. Instead of killing the stranger, the fisherman spoke kindly to him, and invited him to share his evening meal.

The stranger appeared very pleased and ate and drank, but spoke no word at all, The fisherman thought: "He speaks another language."

Quite suddenly the stranger vanished, and only the remains of the meal convinced the fisherman that he had not been dreaming.

The next evening when he went to empty his baskets, he was astonished to find them overflowing with fish. He could not account for his good fortune, and his surprise was even greater when the same thing occurred the next day. On the third day the baskets were again quite full, and when the fisherman came to the last basket he saw that it contained a single monstrous fish.

"Do you not know me?" said the fish.

"Indeed no, Mr. Fish. I have never seen you before!" declared the fisherman, nearly upsetting the canoe in his astonishment.

"Have you forgotten the stranger whom you treated so courteously?" went on the fish. "It was I, and I am the King of the fishes. I am grateful for your kindness and intend to reward you."

Then the fish jumped into the river with a great splash. But ever afterwards the fishing-baskets were full every evening, and the fisherman became rich and prosperous.

---

28. The Ten Goldsmiths

A GOLDSMITH in a small village had ten sons, to all of whom he taught his trade. In time they became skilful craftsmen, and when the old man was dying he called the ten around him and addressed them thus:

"My sons, in this small village there is certainly not enough work for ten goldsmiths. I have therefore decided that the most skilful of you shall remain here in my place, while the rest must go out into the world and seek their fortunes elsewhere."

At this all the sons exclaimed that the plan was good, but who was to say which of them was the most skilful? The old man smiled and answered:

"I have thought of this also. I shall allow you all a month in which to make some article of gold, and at the end of that time I will judge which has been most skilfully executed."

The ten sons immediately set to work to fashion some article, and all displayed great industry during the allotted space of time. At the end of the month they came to their father, as he lay dying on the ground, and placed before him the articles they had made.

One had made a chain of fine gold, every link of which was the perfect shape of an elephant; another had made a knife, beautifully ornamented; another a little casket; another a ring representing serpents twisted together, with shining scales; another a water-pot of pleasing shape; and so on.

The old man smiled with pleasure to see what the industry of his sons had accomplished, but when he counted the articles before him, he found there were only nine. When he found that one of his sons had produced nothing, he was angered, especially when this proved to be the eldest son, whom he had secretly thought to be more skilful than his brothers. After bitterly reproaching this son, whose name was Ayo, for his laziness, the father prepared to give his decision on the work of the other brothers; but Ayo suddenly stepped forward and begged him to wait for another hour before making his choice.

"Meanwhile, Father," said he, "let us sit round the fire all together for the last time, parching corn and telling stories."

This was how the family spent their time in the rainy season, and all gladly consented.

As they seated themselves upon the ground, the father took up a full ripe ear of corn which lay near him. What was his astonishment when he tried to pick the grains to discover that it was made of gold!

For this was what Ayo had made, and he had prepared a little trick to test the perfection of his work. So skilfully was it executed that all had been deceived, thinking it a real ear of corn, and on this account the father and nine brothers all agreed that Ayo's work was certainly the best.

Thus Ayo took his father's place, and the rest set out in different directions to seek their fortune.

---

29. THE COOKING-POT

A MAN once brought home to his wife a very old cooking-pot, and told her to use it every day when preparing the evening meal.

The woman was not pleased at the idea of using such a battered vessel, and feared that her friends would ridicule her, but she dared not disobey her husband, and began to use the pot as he demanded.

Little did she guess that the pot was a magic one, and had the virtue of turning the ashes of the fire, on which it rested, into gold. Every night the husband crept out, when all were asleep in the huts around the compound, and gathered together these golden ashes, which he stored safely away.

One day a young man in the village was about to set off on a journey; he came to the woman while her husband was absent, and asked a favour of her. He said that he had taken a fancy to her old cooking-pot, and would give her a fine new one in exchange for it. The woman hesitated, but she was ashamed of the ugly old pot, and was glad of an excuse to get rid of it.

When her husband found what she had done, he was very angry, and beat her soundly; but it was now too late to recover the pot, as the young man was already far away in the forest. Naturally he had not obtained the pot without knowing its secret, for he had observed the actions of the man who so mysteriously collected the ashes every night; and it is said that from that day the young man spent his life cooking, and so earned the name of "Chop," or "Food"!

30. The Parrot

THERE was a grey parrot which knew how to speak and had the habit of correcting anybody who did not tell the truth.

The parrot was the pet of an untruthful woman, and she found the bird's habit so inconvenient, that she at length decided to get rid of it.

One day a neighbour was passing her house, and the woman called out to him from the threshold to come and see the beautiful tame parrot which she intended to give him as a present.

The man asked her why she desired to part with so beautiful a bird, and to this the woman replied: "Because it eats a great deal, and I am poor."

The parrot cried out. "She lies!"

The neighbour took no notice, thanked the woman, and returned home with the bird on his shoulder. When he reached his house, his wife asked him where he had found the bird.

"As I came through the forest, it flew down and perched on my shoulder," replied the man, but the parrot quickly cried out: "He lies!"

The man soon discovered how awkward it was to have such a truthful pet, and he was often tempted to wring the bird's neck.

It happened that this man was dishonest, and stole a great many articles which he buried in a deep hole, unknown to anybody. He would have been quite secure but for the wonderful parrot.

When the thefts were discovered, a search was made in the man's house, but nothing was found there. The searchers were therefore forced to consider that he was innocent. As they went out, they said to him: "Are you sure you have not stolen these things?"

"I am sure!" said the man indignantly; but the parrot cried out: "He lies!"

The man was so enraged that he seized the bird and twisted its neck, but the suspicion of the searchers was aroused, and eventually they discovered the hole, which was marked with a little stake, and all the stolen articles were found. Had it not been for the truthful parrot, the secret would never have been revealed.

31. THE GHOST-CATCHER

KING ABIPA took a fancy to remove his whole court to a new capital, and for this purpose he decided to build a town on a certain hill which pleased him.

His nobles, however, did not at all desire the change, and some of them met together to make a plan which would turn the King away from his project.

They agreed to send certain slaves of repulsive appearance, whom they possessed, to haunt the hill after the manner of ghosts, so that the King would be afraid to build his capital there. One noble sent a hunchback, another an albino, another a leper, and a fourth a dwarf.

When the King's messengers arrived to survey the hill, they saw these strange apparitions leaping about with torches in their hands, and shouting with one voice: "Ko si aye! Ko si aye!" (No room! No room!).

They returned in terror to the King, and told him that the hill was haunted by ghosts.

However, one of the royal advisers suspected a plot, and advised the King to send hunters to the hill to capture the "ghosts."

The King took this advice, and the hunters returned with the supposed "ghosts," who were, of course, in abject terror at being discovered. Instead of killing them, however, the King kept them hidden and invited all his nobles to a banquet. When they had feasted merrily, he sent round to each noble a calabash of beer by the hands of a slave.

What was the dismay of the four rebellious nobles to receive the calabash, one from his hunchback, another from his albino, and the others from the hands of the leper and the dwarf!

Obviously the plot had been discovered, and all four nobles expected to be put to death for opposing the King; but the wise Abipa said no word about the matter, and the banquet ended in silence.

Soon afterwards the court removed to the new town without any opposition, and henceforth the King was known as "the Ghost-Catcher."

32. Tortoise And The King

ONE year the Elephant had done a great deal of damage, breaking down the trees, drinking up the water in a time of scarcity, and eating the first tender crops from the fields.

The King's hunters tried in vain to destroy him, for Elephant knew many charms, and always escaped from their traps.

At last the King offered the hand of his daughter in marriage to anyone who would rid the country of the pest.

Tortoise went to the palace and offered to catch Elephant, and then made his preparations. Outside the town a large pit was dug, and on the top of it was laid a thin platform covered with velvet cloths and leopard-skins, like a throne.

Then Tortoise set off into the forest, accompanied by slaves and drummers. Elephant was very much surprised to see his little friend Tortoise riding in such state, and suspected a trap; but Tortoise said that the old King was dead and the people all wished Elephant to rule over them, because he was the greatest of all animals. When he heard this, Elephant was flattered, and agreed to accompany Tortoise to the town. But when he went up on to the platform to be crowned King, the wood gave way beneath him, and he crashed down into the pit and was speedily slain by the King's hunters.

All the people rejoiced, and praised the cunning of Tortoise, who went to the palace to receive his bride. But the King refused to give his daughter to such an insignificant creature, and Tortoise determined to have a revenge. When the new crops were just ripening, he called together all the field-mice and elves, and asked them to eat up and carry away the corn. They were only too pleased with the idea, and the farmers in distress found the fields quite bare.

Now there was prospect of a famine in the land, and the King offered the same reward as before to anyone who would rid the country of the pests.

Tortoise once again appeared in the palace and offered his help. The King was eager enough to accept it, but Tortoise cautiously refused to do anything until the Princess became his bride.

The King was thus forced to consent to the marriage, and when it had taken place, Tortoise, true to his word, called together all the mice and elves and showed them a platform loaded with dainty morsels of food. He then addressed them as follows:

"The people are so distressed at the damage you have done, that they have prepared this feast for you, and they promise to do the same twice every year, before the harvesting of the first and second crops, if you will agree not to touch the corn in the fields."

The little creatures all consented, and marched in a great crowd to the platform, which they soon cleared.

The King and his people were not very pleased to hear of this arrangement, but they were so afraid of Tortoise that they could not complain, and after that the mice and elves never troubled the country again.

33. Tortoise And Mr. Fly

ONCE Tortoise and his family fell on hard times and had nothing to eat, but they noticed that their neighbour, Mr. Fly, seemed to be very prosperous and feasted every night.

Tortoise was curious to know how he obtained so much money, and after watching him for some days he discovered that Mr. Fly flew away every morning early with a large empty sack on his back, and returned in the evening with the sack full, and after that his wife would prepare a feast.

One morning Tortoise hid in the sack and waited to see what would happen. Soon Mr. Fly came out of his house, lifted up the sack, and flew away.

He descended at last in the market-place of a large town, where drummers were beating the tones of the dance, and maidens were dancing before a crowd of people.

Mr. Fly laid his sack on the ground, and Tortoise saw him standing beside one of the drummers. When the people threw money, Mr. Fly picked the coins up and hid them in his sack, and by evening he had collected a great quantity. Then he took up the sack again and flew home. Tortoise quickly got out and took most of the money with him, so that poor Mr. Fly was surprised to find the sack almost empty.

This happened several times, until one day as he put money in the sack Mr. Fly caught sight of Tortoise hiding inside it. He was very angry at the trick, and going to the drummer asked him if he had missed any money.

"Yes," said the drummer. "For some days I have been losing coins."

"Look inside this sack," replied Mr. Fly, "and you will see the thief sitting among the money he has stolen."

The drummer peeped inside the sack and saw Tortoise.

"How shall the thief be punished?" he cried angrily.

"Just tie up the sack," said Mr. Fly, "and then beat upon it as if it were a drum."

So the drummer tied up the sack and beat upon it until Tortoise was black and blue, and this is why his back is covered with bruises.

Then Mr. Fly picked up the sack, and flew high up in the air and dropped it. By chance the sack fell down just outside Tortoise's house, and neighbours came to tell Nyanribo, his wife, that someone had left a present outside the door. But when she opened the sack in the presence of a crowd of people, she found only Tortoise inside, more dead than alive. Then Mr. Fly made a song and narrated the whole story, and the drummers also played it, and Tortoise and Nyanribo were so ashamed that they left the place and went to live in another country.

34. Erin And Erinomi (The Land And Water Elephants)

TORTOISE was always fond of making mischief between harmless people. One day as he walked along the river-bank he came upon the Elephant and said to him:

"The Hippo is boasting that you are only a weakling, and that you have not strength to pull a log out of the river."

"That is false!" cried the Elephant, and to prove his strength he allowed Tortoise to tie a strong rope to his trunk and attach the other end to a log in the river.

Tortoise went clown to the water holding the rope, and said to Hippo:

"The Elephant is boasting of his strength, and he declares that you are a weakling and could not pull down a tree."

"That is false!" cried the Hippo. "I can pull down any tree."

Tortoise then said that he had attached his rope to a tree, and would fasten the other end to Hippo's horn. This he did, and the two animals began to pull, one on each end of the rope. Elephant pulled and pulled, and the Hippo pulled and pulled, and neither gave way.

After some time Hippo rested, and Elephant came down to the water to quench his thirst, and then they saw the trick that had been played on them.

Snorting with anger, they began to look for the mischievous Tortoise, but by this time he was, you may be sure, very far away.

35. The Three Deaths Of Tortoise

TORTOISE had many enemies, and they plotted together to kill him.

One night when Tortoise was asleep in his hut, they set fire to it, and as they saw the flames leaping up, they said to one another:

"He cannot escape. He will die."

But Tortoise drew himself into his shell and was untouched by the fire, and in the morning his enemies were astonished to see him walking about as usual.

Soon they made another plan and threw Tortoise into a pool of water.

"The pool is deep. He will drown," said his enemies to one another.

But Tortoise had drawn himself into his shell and was secure, and at noon the sun shone fiercely and dried up the pool.

That evening Tortoise walked about the village as if nothing had happened, and his enemies were astonished.

The next day they made a third attempt to kill him. They made a deep hole in the ground and buried Tortoise, and this time they were quite sure he could not escape. To mark the place, they put a bamboo stake in the ground.

Meanwhile a man who was passing saw the bamboo stake, and thought, "Someone has buried a treasure here!" He called his friends, and they began to dig, but all they found was Tortoise fast asleep inside his shell.

Tortoise walked about the village again, looking very happy, and his enemies were filled with astonishment.

"He has a charm, and we shall never be able to kill him," they said to one another, and from that day they left him in peace.

36. TORTOISE AND THE COCK

ONE day Tortoise and Nyanribo felt very hungry, but they could not afford to buy food, and while they were discussing what might be done, Tortoise heard a cock crowing, and it gave him an idea. He went to the cock and said:

"I have come to warn you. I heard the farmer asking his wife to prepare chicken for dinner to-morrow."

At this all the fowls were in great distress and wondered which of them was to be killed.

Tortoise replied:

"I heard the farrner's wife say that she will kill the first of you which she hears crowing or clucking in the morning."

Naturally the fowls decided to be absolutely silent.

Very early in the moming Tortoise went creeping among the fowls and stole all the eggs from the nests, taking them one by one to his house; but the cock was afraid to crow and the hens were afraid to cluck, and when the farmer's wife came to collect the eggs, she found that they had all been stolen.

At this she flew into a rage, and killed all the fowls instead of one, and while the farmer and his wife had a feast of chicken, Tortoise and Nyanribo invited their friends to a feast of eggs!

37. Tortoise And Crab

EVERYONE knows that Tortoise and Crab are enemies.

One morning on the seashore they decided to fight to see which was the stronger, but, as both of them are protected by a hard shell, neither could succeed in injuring the other.

Finally they came to an agreement that they were equal in strength.

"We are so well protected by our armour," said Tortoise, "that no one can harm us."

"And thus," said Crab, "we are the strongest creatures in the world."

But at this moment a boy passed by and picked them both up. Tortoise was boiled in a pot and his shell was made into ornaments, while Crab was cooked in a stew for the boy's supper. Since that day the descendants of the two boasters have always been ashamed to meet, and that is why they always shun one another.

38. Tortoise And Pigeon

TORTOISE and Pigeon were often seen walking together, but unfortunately Tortoise treated his friend rather badly, and often played tricks on him. Pigeon never complained, and put up with everything in a good-humoured way. Once Tortoise came to him and said:

"I am going on a journey to-day to visit my cousins; will you come with me?"

Pigeon agreed to accompany him, and they set off. When they had go ne some distance they came to a river, and Pigeon was forced to take Tortoise upon his back and fly across with him.

Soon afterwards they reached the house of Tortoise's cousins. Tortoise left his friend standing at the door while he went inside and greeted his relatives. They had prepared a feast for him, and they all began to eat together.

"Will you not ask your friend to eat with us?" said the cousins; but Tortoise was so greedy that he did not wish Pigeon to share the feast, and replied:

"My friend is a silly fellow, he will not eat in a stranger's house, and he is so shy that he refuses to come in."

After some time Tortoise bade farewell to his cousins, saying, "Greetings to you on your hospitality," and came out of the house. But Pigeon, who was both tired and hungry, had heard his words and determined to pay him out for once.

When they reached the river-bank, he took Tortoise up once again on his back; when he had flown half-way across, he allowed Tortoise to fall off into the river. But, by chance, instead of falling into the water, he landed on the back of a crocodile which was floating on the surface, and when the crocodile came up to the bank, Tortoise quickly descended and hurried away.

Pigeon saw what had happened, and that Tortoise had safely reached the land; so he flew ahead of him until he came to a field where a dead horse was lying.

To trick Tortoise once more, Pigeon cut off the horse's head and stuck it in the ground, as if it grew there like a plant.

When Tortoise reached the field and saw the horse's head, he went straight away to the King of the country and told him that he knew of a place where horses' heads grew like plants.

"If this is true," said the King, "I will reward you with a great treasure; but if it is false, you must die."

The King and a large crowd of people accompanied Tortoise to the field, but meanwhile Pigeon had removed the head. Tortoise ran about looking for it, but in vain, and he was condemned to die. A large fire was made, and Tortoise was thrown on to it.

But now Pigeon repented of the trick he had done, and quickly called together all the birds of the air. They came like a wind, beating out the fire with their wings, and so rescued Tortoise.

When Pigeon had explained this trick, the King pardoned Tortoise, and allowed the two friends to depart in safety.

---

39. Tortoise And The Whip-Tree

THERE was a famine in the land, and everyone longed for food. Each day Tortoise went into the forest to see if he could find anything to eat, but in the evenings he came home discouraged with only a few herbs and dried-up nut-kernels for his family.

One day, as he walked through a grove, he saw two trees close together—a small stunted tree and a big tree with thick foliage and spreading branches. "What sort of tree are you?" he asked the little tree.

"I am the Chop-tree," was the reply.

"Well, Chop-tree, what can you produce?" asked Tortoise. And at the words the little tree waved its branches and a shower of food fell to the ground. Tortoise ate until nothing remained, and then turned to the tall and handsome tree.

"And what tree are you?" he asked, thinking that such a splendid tree must produce rich fruit. The tree told him that its name was Whip-tree, to which Tortoise replied: "Whip-tree, what can you produce?"

At these words the Whip-tree bent its branches and beat Tortoise until he cried for mercy. When the beating ceased, Tortoise went home, but, being of a greedy nature, he said nothing of the two trees, and showed his wife only a few poor nuts which he had found.

After that he went every day to the Chop-tree and feasted to his heart's content. While his family and all the people, even to the King, became thin and meagre, Tortoise appeared daily fatter and more prosperous, until Nyanribo, his wife, began to suspect.

One day Nyanribo resolved to follow him into the forest, and great was her surprise when she saw her husband stand under the little tree and say: "Tree, do your duty!" The branches waved, and rich titbits fell to the ground.

Nyanribo cried out in astonishment and reproached her husband for his greediness. She hastened back to the town and returned with the whole family of children and cousins. She stood under the Chop-tree and said: "Tree, do your duty!"

When the food fell down, they all partook of the feast.

But spiteful Tortoise was displeased, and exclaimed:

"I wish you would stand under the other tree and receive your proper reward!"

Hearing this, they all went to stand under the Whip-tree, and Nyanribo again cried: "Tree, do your duty!" Alas! The branches began to beat them all soundly until they died.

Tortoise was alarmed at this and hastily returned to his house, but the neighbours soon noticed that his wife and family were absent, and the King ordered Tortoise to account for their disappearance.

Tortoise therefore led the King and all the nobles and the people into the forest, and when they were gathered under the Chop-tree he cried out: "Tree, do your duty!" and, as before, a feast appeared, which the hungry people soon devoured.

Tortoise then asked them to stand underneath the othet tree, and this they were eager to do. The King himself was the one to cry out: "Tree, do your duty!" and the branches began to beat all those who stood below until they cried out with pain.

In a great rage the people hunted for Tortoise, desiring to kill him; but he hid inside his shell, in a secret place, and they could not harm him.

He stayed in concealment until the King died and a new King was found, and then he thought it safe to appear in the town. But whenever he hears the two words "Chop" and "Whip," he hides in his shell, thinking himself in danger.

40. Tortoise And The Rain

TORTOISE and a Cloud once made the following agreement: Whenever Tortoise very much desired fine weather, he was to stand outside his house and call: "Pass! Pass!" and then the Cloud would roll away and allow the sun to shine. And when Tortoise desired rain, he was to cry: "Fall! Fall!" and the rain would pour down. In payment for this service, Tortoise was to place on the ground each time a certain number of cowries.

Tortoise was delighted with this arrangement, and at first he duly placed the sum of money on the ground every time he asked the Cloud for fine or wet weather.

One day, the occasion of a Chief's wedding, the sky was very cloudy, and it seemed likely to rain. Tortoise heard the Chief complaining: "We have promised the drummers a great deal of money, but if it rains nobody will come to see the maidens dance at my wedding!"

Tortoise went to the Chief and said: "If you will give me a certain sum, I will hold up the clouds on my hard back and there will be no rain."

The Chief readily agreed to pay the cowries Tortoise demanded, and Tortoise stood at the back of his hut and cried to the Cloud: "Pass! Pass!" The Cloud rolled back, the sun shone brightly, and the wedding took place with much rejoicing.

But Tortoise did not lay any money on the ground, and instead, he kept the whole amount for himself.

The next day a man came to Tortoise's house and offered him much money if he would cause the rain to fall. "For," he said, "my fishing-stakes are too high, but if it rains the river will swell and the fish will come into my baskets."

"Very well," replied Tortoise. "I will throw a spear into the clouds, and the rain will fall."

Then he stood at the back of his house, where he could not be seen, and cried to the Cloud: "Fall! Fall!" It began to pour with rain.

But again he neglected to lay money on the ground and kept it all for himself. Soon, in this way, he grew rich and famous, and almost every day someone asked for fine or rainy weather. He stored many bags of cowries in his house and gave nothing to the Cloud.

When two people asked him for rain and sunshine on the same day, Tortoise pretended that he had grown tired with holding up the clouds on his back, and so the rain fell.

But after some time, seeing how rich Tortoise became, the hard-working Cloud was angry and decided to punish him.

One day Tortoise wished to set out on a journey with his family, so he stood outside his house and cried: "Pass! Pass! Let the sun shine on my journey!"

But as soon as he had set out, the Cloud rolled back again and rain poured down in torrents, causing a great flood in which Tortoise and all his family were drowned.